ASTROLOGY

The Modern Mystic Library

The Dream Book

Reading Tea Leaves

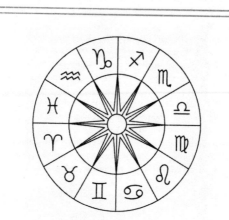

ASTROLOGY

The Modern Mystic's Guide
to the Stars

SEPHARIAL

Foreword by June Rifkin

ST. MARTIN'S
ESSENTIALS
NEW YORK

Published in the United States by St. Martin's Essentials,
an imprint of St. Martin's Publishing Group

ASTROLOGY. Foreword copyright © 2022 by June Rifkin. All rights reserved.
Printed in the United States of America. For information, address
St. Martin's Publishing Group, 120 Broadway, New York, NY 10271.

www.stmartins.com

Library of Congress Cataloging-in-Publication Data

Names: Sepharial, 1864–1929, author.
Title: Astrology : the modern mystic's guide to the stars / Sepharial.
Description: First St. Martin's Essentials. | New York : St. Martin's
    Essentials, [2022] | Series: The modern mystic library
Identifiers: LCCN 2022020120 | ISBN 9781250861948 (trade paperback) |
    ISBN 9781250861955 (ebook)
Subjects: LCSH: Astrology—Handbooks, manuals, etc.
Classification: LCC BF1701 .S474 2022 | DDC 133.5—dc23/eng/20220613
LC record available at https://lccn.loc.gov/2022020120

Our books may be purchased in bulk for promotional, educational,
or business use. Please contact your local bookseller or the Macmillan
Corporate and Premium Sales Department at 1-800-221-7945, extension 5442, or by email
at MacmillanSpecialMarkets@macmillan.com.

This book is an updated and condensed edition of *Astrology* by Sepharial.
The original was first published in 1920.

First St. Martin's Essentials Edition: 2022

10   9   8   7   6   5   4   3   2   1

CONTENTS

SECTION I:
THE ALPHABET OF THE HEAVENS

CONTENTS

SECTION II:
HOW TO READ A HOROSCOPE

SECTION III:
THE STARS IN THEIR COURSES

CONTENTS

PUBLISHER'S NOTE

In recent years, astrology has enjoyed a renaissance in popularity, but it has much deeper, older roots. As you'll read in the following pages, ancient civilizations were also fascinated by the planets and their effects on us. The book you're reading is a little bit more recent than the Babylonians. Originally written in 1920 by Sepharial, the much catchier pen name of Walter Gorn Old, this book is a classic of astrology that has stood the test of time.

In this new edition, the language of the book has been updated throughout and we've omitted the sections and tables that the original readers used to create their own natal charts. These days, instead of lugging out your ephemeris, a compass and ruler, and all the math you remember from high school, you can simply download a copy of your natal chart online. (The resources section at the end of the book will point you to specific websites.) Advances in technology notwithstanding, Sepharial's guide is an insightful and comprehensive introduction that will help you begin to unravel the mysteries of astrology. Enjoy your venture into the secrets of the stars!

FOREWORD

Astrology shows us how the placement of the stars and planets can influence our lives and the world around us. Examining our birth chart—a cosmic snapshot of where the stars and planets were situated in the sky at the exact time and place of our birth—provides a unique glimpse into our personality, talents, potential, and challenges. This information can be an excellent tool for self-discovery. It can validate what we already know about ourselves and our character—not just the good things but also those traits we may not readily recognize, or prefer to ignore or deny. Every chart contains a blend of positive and challenging traits, but having this awareness helps us identify and navigate personal obstacles we confront on our life path. In an era in which humankind is seeking greater self-awareness and a clearer sense of purpose, our horoscope can be a valuable reference point on the journey through life.

Although the origins of astrology can be traced to ancient Chinese, Indian, and Babylonian texts dating as far back as 2000 BC, interest in astrology has ebbed and flowed, depending on the era. For example, it was considered heresy during the Middle Ages, yet enlightening during the Renaissance. In more recent history, astrology saw a revival in the late nineteenth and early twentieth centuries and then another decline until the late 1960s. The sixties were a remarkably progressive time of peace, love, sex, drugs, and rock and roll—when astrology reemerged to be embraced by youth culture and the release of one of the most popular astrology books ever, *Linda Goodman's Sun Signs*. As the first astrology book to make the *New York Times* best-seller list, it was groundbreaking in its comprehensive focus on each zodiac sign and had substantial global reach. Millions of copies were sold, making astrology mainstream and paving the way for other books to come.

While the popularity of astrology ebbed again

before the turn of the twenty-first century, the internet shifted the tide. Savvy astrologers expanded their public reach through websites, blogs, podcasts, YouTube videos, and mobile apps. These practitioners gained even more significant ground when the onset of a global pandemic crossed the growing discomfort of political polarization. The fear and anxiety that ensued from these events moved many people to reassess their life or explore their true purpose. They sought to regain their footing by seeking knowledge about their future and the world at large. Whether through personal readings or the study of astrology via online classes and books, many people began turning to astrology for personal enlightenment and a way to navigate a rapidly changing and unpredictable world.

Taking a deep dive into astrology can be a refuge when dealing with personal challenges, grief, or uncertainty. Reading a monthly forecast or the latest planetary transits gives us a sneak preview of what's to come, prepares us for the worst, and provides hope for the best. Every book on astrology takes a slightly different approach to the subject in terms of perspective and tone. Yet, more often than not, there are significant parallels and overlap of content. The eager student or hobbyist may read multiple titles to build knowledge and intuitively develop their own approach.

When the first edition of this classic book (previously subtitled *How to Make and Read Your Own Horoscope*) was published in 1920, crafting a natal chart was complex and time-consuming. You would need several resources at hand: a birth certificate; an ephemeris (a book listing the positions of planets); a Table of Houses; a compass and ruler with which to draw a chart; paper and pencils; a dash of math savvy; and a whole lot of patience. This dedication to the process was undertaken mainly by those passionate about astrology, because who else would devote the time?

Nowadays, technology makes it possible to pop in some data on a form, and voilà—a birth chart appears seconds later. In addition, some websites not only create charts but also offer a free (albeit generic, computer-generated) natal report that will likely satisfy the average person's curiosity. However, for those interested in exploring a more personalized analysis of their chart or the charts of others close to them, reaching for comprehensive primers on astrology will prove richer and more satisfying. And while the characteristics of the signs, the planets, and the houses they occupy have remained largely consistent over centuries—except for Pluto, which wasn't discovered until 1930 and therefore not yet included—time-honored texts like this provide a unique perspective on ways to analyze and interpret a natal chart.

The author of *Astrology*, Sepharial, is the pen name of Walter Gorn Old, a respected British astrologer and prolific writer of the late nineteenth and early twentieth centuries who published more than sixty books and articles on astrology and other occult-oriented subjects. He was an active member of the Theosophical Society, founded to study and explore psychic and spiritual phenomena. He was also a member of several astrological societies in the United Kingdom and the United States. Sepharial's reputation and broad reach made astrology accessible to the masses through the columns and horoscopes he contributed to several periodicals. He was a pioneer in spearheading the sun sign horoscopes we regularly see in newspapers and magazines. However, his books and articles were quite sophisticated and esoteric, geared more to the serious student of astrology.

This volume you are about to read focuses on what Sepharial classifies as *genethliacal astrology*—in simple terms, natal astrology. His objective is to explain how anyone's birth chart can be examined to reveal "the complex nature of human character and the causes behind the myriad ways it expresses itself." Further, he hopes that readers will discover what an enlightening and helpful tool it is and be intrigued enough to pursue the study of astrology.

Many popular astrology books published over the last fifty years have placed significant attention on the attributes of each sign of the zodiac. In contrast, Sepharial groups the sun signs together by modality (cardinal, fixed, mutable) and focuses more on the placement of planets and houses in a natal chart to create an overall picture of a person's strengths, vulnerabilities, and potentials in all areas of life.

Given the modest size of this volume, Sepharial delivers his knowledge succinctly. His style is scholarly and sharp. He knows his subject well and conveys it with confidence and conviction. He doesn't mince words when describing the more challenging or darker elements at play. Although today's readers may be taken aback by the often bleak interpretations of various house placements and planetary aspects shown in a natal chart, this approach can actually call attention to tendencies, behaviors, or potential health vulnerabilities we may be unaware of—or else prefer to avoid or deny altogether. While Sepharial wholeheartedly believes that a birth chart is an accurate blueprint of one's life and character, he also admits that genetics, family life, and upbringing can alter the cosmic path of personal health, relationships, finances, and success.

On a personal note, my initial introduction to astrology came about when I was a young teenager, reading horoscopes in whatever magazines I had at home or perused at friends' houses or the dental office. I had no idea what it meant to be a Pisces (my birth sign). I only knew from reading teen magazines that George Harrison, "the quiet Beatle," was a Pisces, too.

One day, a friend surprised me with an annual Pisces wall calendar—she thought the gift would be a fun way to start off the new year. I was in the throes of middle school, which was an already awkward time made worse by my struggles in math class. My mother, concerned about my plunging grades, enlisted the help of my math teacher, a kindly older gentleman, who agreed to tutor me weekly after school. As my grasp of algebra evolved, so did our friendship—one that lasted into adulthood—and he became a trusted mentor. So, when I opened the calendar that January and read the general personality traits of Pisces, I was stunned by the line, "Pisces women love music, movies, daydreaming, and hanging out with their math teachers." The music, movies, and daydreaming? That was definitely true yet could apply to *anyone,* not just a Pisces. But the quirky math teacher reference? Too eerily accurate. I was utterly astounded and then fascinated. And that cosmic coincidence sparked my interest in astrology, which continues to this day. (Thankfully, no math is necessary.)

No matter how you were introduced to astrology— through a friend, an article, a post on social media, or a horoscope that rang all too true—may the following pages help you better understand your natal chart and navigate its potential.

June Rifkin
Co-author, *The Complete Book of Astrology* and
The One World Tarot

PREFACE TO THE REVISED AND ENLARGED EDITION 1920

Since this book was first published, the amount of interest in the topic of astrology has created an increased demand for a small book of practical astrology designed for beginners. I believe this new, expanded revision of the original edition will be even more popular with those who are just beginning to explore the world of astrology.

The practical uses of astrology are recognized and appreciated more every day, and although some of the more complex developments in astrology are not included in this book, hopefully this small volume will encourage readers to pursue the study of this arcane and little-known science. In doing so, you will discover for yourself, without any prompting on my part, that astrology is a practical and useful tool.

There are, of course, many aspects of this fascinating subject not discussed in this book, which focuses solely on Genethliacal Astrology, or the Doctrine of Nativities. But if it's true, as I believe, that "the proper study for mankind is man," then this is undoubtedly the first area of astrology to focus your attention on.

When we understand the complex nature of human character and the causes behind the myriad ways it expresses itself, once we have seen how the many-colored dome of Life overarches and guides our sublunary world with its kaleidoscope of forces, we will be better equipped to deal with human nature as we encounter it. We will also be able to direct our thoughts and attention to build a better world by channeling our natural passions and powers into useful forms.

To study the true nature of oneself, to find the line of least resistance, to discover the measure of your own soul in the universe, and the extent and limit of your own ambition—these are all things we must know, and that astrology can reveal to us.

Apart from the scientific truths that astrology

shares with us, there are other, no less important or fascinating, truths of a purely philosophical nature that will inevitably shape our thoughts and ideas about the purpose of life. Astrology gives students an entirely new lens through which to view the deeper problems of existence. **Astrology is a revelation, an enlightenment, and a conviction.**

—SEPHARIAL

INTRODUCTION

From the earliest days of history, the subject of astrology has interested the minds of a unique group of thinkers. The science has never been universally accepted, though with its countless adherents in the East and the ever-increasing number of its advocates in the West, we can safely say there is no faith more universal than the belief that the heavenly bodies influence the destinies of human beings. Within the limits of this small book, it's not possible to adequately reconcile the paradox between Freewill and the governing force of the heavens. However, it's obvious that the concept is not altogether unscientific. We can speak of the "free path of vibration" for particles while at the same time knowing that these atoms have restricted characteristics, modes of motion, etc., and are all subject to the general laws of physics and chemistry. If we can trace a connection between the locations of the heavenly bodies at the moment of a person's birth and the life and character of that person, along with an exact correlation between the course of events in that person's life and movement of the planets after their birth, we should accept that fact for what it's worth and arrange our philosophical notions accordingly.

As far back as the year B.C. 2154, we find mention of the importance Chinese rulers attached to celestial phenomena. It's recorded in the Historical Classic of China that two of the court astronomers once neglected their duty so that when, on the tenth of October, there was a great eclipse of the Sun between seven and nine o'clock in the morning the people were wholly unprepared for it. For this offense, the astrologers were stripped of their offices and exiled. In India, we find the classical writers Garga, Parashara, and Mihira, together with their legions of commentators. The Assyrian records are full of astrological allusions regarding the influence of planetary conjunctions and stellar positions. Greek mythology is nothing but a vast system of cosmographical astrology, and you can find the origins of the stories in the constellations of the heavens and the corresponding evolution of the human race. Aristotle made it a part of his philosophy. Hipparchus, Hippocrates, Thales, Galenius, and others believed in its principles. We are indebted to Claudius Ptolemy for the first concise and scientific statement of astrology's principles and practice in the European tradition. He wrote the *Tetrabiblos,* or *Four Books,* and laid the foundations of a true astrological science. Julius Firmicus confirmed Ptolemy and enlarged on his observations. The subsequent discovery of the planets Uranus and Neptune by Herschel and Adams widened the field of research and gave later astrologers the clues to understanding much of what had not been understood before.

These discoveries did not overturn the whole system of astrology, as some have imagined and foolishly stated, nor did they negate the conclusions drawn from observing the seven bodies that made up the previously known solar system. But their discovery made it possible to fill in the blank spaces and to account for certain events that could not be accounted for by the known planets. The discovery of argon did not destroy our conclusions regarding the nature and characteristics of oxygen or hydrogen or nitrogen, nor give an entirely new meaning to the word "atmosphere." Even if seven new planets in our solar system were suddenly to be discovered, there isn't a single paragraph in this book that would need to be revised. What we know about planetary action in human life we know with great certainty, and the effects of one planet can never be confused with those of another.

Incomplete as it must needs be, astrology is a veritable science in its principles and practice. It claims a place among the sciences because it is capable of mathematical demonstration, and deals only with the observed positions and motions of the heavenly bodies. Anyone who holds to the laws of Newton, the solidarity of the solar system, the interaction of the planetary bodies and their electrostatic effects on the Earth, cannot deny the foundational principles of astrology. The application of these principles to the facts of everyday life has been the focus of prolonged research and study for thousands of years around the world. To put astrology to the test all you need to do is create your horoscope.

I know that the present-day study of astrology is

wide-spread, but many are reluctant to acknowledge their interest, for, as Prof. F. Max Müller recently said, "Great is the ignorance which confounds a science requiring the highest education, with that of the ordinary fortune-teller." The science that the great Kepler was compelled "by his unfailing experience of the course of events in harmony with the changes taking place in the heavens" to have "an unwilling belief" in, the science practiced and advocated by Tycho Brahe, the art that arrested the attention of the young Newton and set him pondering on the problems of force and matter, which fascinated the minds of Francis Bacon, Archbishop Usher, Haley, Sir George Witchell, Flamstead, and a host of others, is today the favorite interest of thousands of intelligent minds and will become a popular subject.

This book will be useful to those who are looking to make an initial study of the science of horoscopy. Though it by no means exhausts all there is to know about the subject, the material in these pages is an accurate and reliable place to begin and will allow anyone to test the claims of astrology themselves.

THE ALPHABET OF
THE HEAVENS

THE PLANETS

We begin our exploration of the heavens with the planets themselves. The luminaries (Sun and Moon) and planets are known to astronomers under the following names and symbols:

The Sun ☉

Moon ☽

Neptune ♆

Uranus ♅

Saturn ♄

Jupiter ♃

Mars ♂

Venus ♀
Mercury ☿

Neptune revolves around the Sun in its distant orbit once in about one hundred and sixty-five years. Uranus completes its orbital revolution in eighty-four years, Jupiter in twelve years, Mars in about fifteen months, Venus in eleven months, and Mercury in eighteen weeks. If you imagine these bodies to be revolving in a plane around the Sun with you standing in the center of the Sun, the movement of the planets will appear almost uniform and always in one direction. If the orbits of the planets were circular and the Sun was placed in the center of the circle, their motions would be constant. But planetary orbits are elliptical, and the Sun is located in one of the foci of each ellipse. Because of this, a planet's distance from the Sun varies as it moves along its orbit. When a planet is farthest from the Sun, at the far end of its elliptical orbit, is it said to be in **aphelion.** Similarly, when a planet is at the opposite point of its orbit, and is closest to the Sun, this is called the **perihelion.** When at aphelion the planets move slightly slower, and when at perihelion they move slightly quicker. The Earth follows the exact same laws as all other bodies in our solar system.

If, instead of imagining the solar system from the vantage point of the Sun, we consider how the sky appears from Earth (imagining that it is stationary in space and is the center around which the other planets revolve), we will notice several variations in the movements of the planets. From this vantage point, Mercury and Venus will appear to revolve around the Sun, while the Sun itself seems to revolve around the Earth. Sometimes these two planets will appear to lie between the Earth and the Sun, which is called an **Inferior conjunction,** and sometimes they will appear to be on the far side of the sun, known as **Superior conjunction.** At other times Mercury and Venus will appear to the right or left of the Sun, which is known as **East or West elongation.** The other planets, which have orbits that are far larger than Earth's, will appear to revolve around Earth at constantly changing distances and velocities. At certain points in their orbits, they will appear to remain stationary in the same part of the zodiac.

When a planet is called **direct,** this means it is moving forward at its normal speed from our perspective on Earth. In contrast, **retrograde** refers to a planet that appears to be moving *backward* across the sky due to differences in its velocity and Earth's.

The illustration on the following page will help you create a visual image.

G represents our perspective from the earth, with the sun located in the middle. The letter **M** is Mercury when at Inferior conjunction with the Sun as seen from Earth, meaning it appears to be between the Earth and the Sun.

The letter **V** is the planet Venus at Superior conjunction with the Sun, meaning it appears to be on the far side of the Sun.

The points **W** and **E** are the points of greatest elongation West and East, and the letter **S** shows the points in the orbit at which those bodies appear to be stationary when viewed from the Earth, (**G**). As seen from the Earth, Venus would appear to be **direct,** and Mercury **retrograde.**

Because we think of the Earth as the subject of the other planets' influence, in astrology we place it at the center of the field of activity, even though the planets physically revolve around the Sun. If we were making a horoscope for an inhabitant of the planet Mars, we would make Mars the

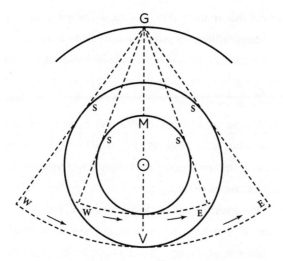

center of the system. So astrology uses a geocentric (Earth-centered) approach instead of a heliocentric (Sun-centered) one.

The Nature of the Planets

Each of the planets has a "personality," and by getting to know their individual influence, we can learn to evaluate their effects when they are working together in concert.

Neptune acts on the human mind to create a high-strung, nervous temperament that can result in great genius or in instability. It creates complications in business and other involved or complicated situations. It influences one towards fraud, double-dealing, and irresponsible actions. In the body it produces a gaunt frame and weak lungs.

Uranus creates an eccentric mind, waywardness, originality, inventiveness. In business, it produces sudden and unexpected developments, irregularities, instability, and a mix of good and bad fortune. In the body, it's related to the nervous system, and its diseases are paralysis, lesions or ulcers, and nerve issues.

Saturn produces a thoughtful, sober, dignified mind; steadfastness, patience, and endurance; along with a disposition to routine and habit. In financial affairs it gives steady results that are equivalent to the effort exerted and success that is slow but sure, but also hardship, lack, and difficulty. In the body it is related to the bones, and its effects are brought about by blockages, chills, and inhibition of function.

Jupiter gives joviality, optimism, bountifulness, generosity, a rich and fruitful mind. It renders the subject fortunate in their affairs, giving success and often wealth. When this planet is a strong presence in the horoscope a person is never out of luck. In the body it is related to the arteries and blood flow, and its diseases are those that are a result of excess, over-indulgence, and congestion.

Mars confers a sense of freedom, ambition and executive ability, frankness, honesty, and a disregard for consequences. It renders the mind forceful and militant, inclined to pursue new projects and ideas. In the body it is related to the muscular system. Its diseases are those associated with inflammation.

Venus confers poetry, good taste, refinement, artistic sense, gentleness, docility, and a love of pleasure. It renders business both pleasant and prosperous, creating profit from both artistic and practical pursuits. Next to Jupiter it has the most positive effects. In the body it is related to the venous system, and its diseases are blood related: eczema, smallpox, measles, etc.

Mercury renders its subjects active, versatile, capable and business-like, disposed to commerce, whether of the mind or the market, eager in the pursuit of knowledge; alert, and well-informed. Its influence on daily life is variable because it always translates the nature of that planet that it is most near. In the body it is related to the senses and to the reflexes.

The Moon gives charisma and gracefulness, an

adaptable nature, variableness, love of change, romance, and adventure; a love for exploration and travel. In the body it corresponds to the glandular system, and its diseases are related to the lymphatic glands and vascular tissue.

The Sun makes its subjects magnanimous, noble, proud, honest and disdainful of immoral actions; loyal, truthful, and fearless. It produces honor and success for officials, and makes the subject fortunate in their affairs. In the body it controls the life force.

Appearance and the Planets

Planetary influence creates very distinct types of people. Their primary features are:

Neptune—Thin, nervous-looking people with thin and usually long faces, frequently wearing a strained or startled look.

Uranus—Tall, wiry, and energetic figures, alert, muscular, erratic, and with a touch of eccentricity.

Saturn—Lean people with deep-set eyes and a heavy brow.

Jupiter—Full bodied, robust, expressive eyes, arched brows, high foreheads, and oval faces.

Mars—Strong, muscular, and athletic bodies, prominent brows, and usually some mark or scar on the face.

Sun—Fresh, clear complexion, round head, broad shoulders, strong jaws, upright and dignified carriage.

Venus—Elegant, well-groomed, and often delicate-looking people, bright eyes, fine teeth and fingernails, small feet, and short fleshy hands.

Mercury—Thin, tall, and active bodies, alert appearance, long arms, and slender hands. Frequently great talkers and quick walkers.

Moon—Rather short and fleshy people, fine teeth, broad chest, and a tendency toward a round or square figure.

Take a look at people as they pass you in the street and consider these types. Simply knowing each planet's nature gives you a key to understanding a bit of their character and destiny.

THE SIGNS OF THE ZODIAC

The **zodiac** is an imaginary circle of sky through which the Sun and planets move in their apparent revolutions round the Earth. It extends from 23° 27′ above the plane of the Equator and the same distance below, bound by the Tropic of Cancer on the North and by the Tropic of Capricorn on the South. **The Ecliptic** is the plane of the Earth's orbit around the Sun or, as it appears from Earth, the path the Sun takes across the celestial sphere. The Ecliptic transects the imaginary circle of the zodiac at an angle of 23° 27′ to the plane of the Equator. The points where it cuts the Equator are called the Equinoxes—the Spring or vernal equinox and the Fall or autumnal equinox.

Understanding a Star Chart

When reading a horoscope, you will see a circular chart that represents the movements of the sun and planets as if they are viewed from Earth. On a natal chart, the horizontal axis, or Ascendant/Descendant axis, represents the horizon line. The Sun and all the planets rise at the **Ascendant** and move clockwise until they set at the **Descendant**. The **Midheaven** (or Medium Coeli, M.C. in latin) and Nadir (or Imum Coeli, I.C.) axis mark the highest and lowest points of the Sun's orbit.

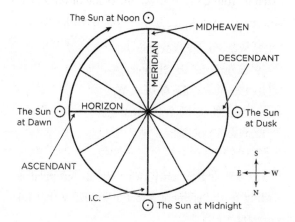

The Zodiac

The Ecliptic is divided into twelve equal sections, counting from the Vernal Equinox. These are called the **Signs of the Zodiac.** Each sign occupies 30 degrees of the circle.

Their names and symbols are as follows:

1. Aries, the Ram ♈
2. Taurus, the Bull ♉
3. Gemini, the Twins ♊
4. Cancer, the Crab ♋
5. Leo, the Lion ♌
6. Virgo, the Virgin ♍
7. Libra, the Balance ♎
8. Scorpio, the Scorpion ♏
9. Sagittarius, the Hunter ♐
10. Capricorn, the Goat ♑
11. Aquarius, the Waterman ♒
12. Pisces, the Fishes ♓

For astrological purposes they are grouped according to the element and the modality that they represent, so:

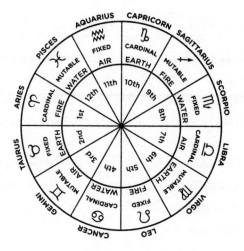

Elements

Fire—Aries, Leo, Sagittarius.

Earth—Taurus, Virgo, Capricorn.

Air—Gemini, Libra, Aquarius.

Water—Cancer, Scorpio, Pisces.

Modality

Cardinal—Aries, Cancer, Libra, Capricorn.

Fixed—Taurus, Leo, Scorpio, Aquarius.

Mutable—Gemini, Virgo, Sagittarius, Pisces.

Every alternate sign, beginning with Aries, is male, and the rest are female. Aries, male; Taurus, female; Gemini, male; Cancer, female, etc. The signs Aries, Leo, and Capricorn are called barren, while Taurus, Cancer, Scorpio, and Pisces are fruitful. Aries governs the East, Cancer the North, Libra the West, and Capricorn the South.

The Double-bodied signs are Gemini, Sagittarius, and Pisces. These classifications are all an important part of astrology and are frequently used in reading a horoscope.

The Influence of the Zodiac

Each of the signs has a particular influence over the people who are born "under" it. A person is considered to be under a sign, that is under its influence, when that sign was rising in the East at the moment of their birth (at the cusp of the First House, see page 28). This is also known as the **rising sign** or **ascendant.** You'll recognize these types among your friends and family:

Aries produces a person with a lean body, long

neck, and high cheekbones. The front teeth are usually large and prominent.

Taurus gives a full, thick-set body, strong neck and shoulders, and round, bullet-shaped head. The hands and feet are short and fleshy.

Gemini produces a tall, active, and upright body, long arms and legs, rather wide shoulders, and thin body.

Cancer denotes a rather short, squat figure, with a full body, round face, full chest, short, fleshy hands and feet.

Leo renders its subjects tall, broad-shouldered, with a robust figure, small round head, and an upright carriage.

Virgo renders the body thin and active, with broad shoulders. Someone who looks like an intellectual or artist.

Libra creates an elegant body, well-developed limbs, fine oval face, beautiful complexion. Some of the most beautiful people fall under this sign.

Scorpio gives a short, thick-set, and powerful figure, broad, deep chest, strong and rather bowed legs.

Sagittarius creates a tall person with a well-made figure, long limbs, rather long face, expressive eyes, and a long nose.

Capricorn produces a slight person, a long and thin neck, prominent features, narrow chin, weak limbs and chest and sloping shoulders. Frequently they are wiry and look as if they are capable of great endurance. The face is thin and hard-set.

Aquarius is the most beautiful after Libra. A tall figure, well-formed with a clear complexion, well-developed chin, and fine, clear forehead.

Pisces produces one of rather short stature, with short limbs and small hands and feet.

The short signs are Taurus, Cancer, Capricorn, and Pisces. The tall signs are Gemini, Leo, Sagittarius, and Aquarius. The others are of medium height.

In addition to the effect of the signs, the planets that are rising in each sign will also affect a person based on their own characteristics. Thus, a person with Cancer as their rising sign (who is "under" Cancer) will be affected differently if the Mars is rising or Venus. The character of the rising planet will combine with and alter the character of the rising sign, so both must be considered together.

Ruling Planets

Each zodiac sign has a **ruling planet,** and the position of the ruling planet of the rising sign has a lot to do with a person's physical appearance. So, if an individual's rising sign is Taurus and its ruling planet, Venus, is in Leo, that person will exhibit some of the traits of a Leo, making them more likely to be tall than Taurus would alone. It is very rare for a person to purely exhibit the characteristics of their rising sign.

The rulership of the planets in the signs is as follows:

Saturn governs Aquarius and Capricorn.
Jupiter governs Pisces and Sagittarius.
Mars governs Aries and Scorpio.
Venus governs Taurus and Libra.
Mercury governs Gemini and Virgo.
The Moon governs Cancer.
The Sun governs Leo.

When a planet is moving through the section of the zodiac relating to a sign that it governs, its influence is stronger than usual. When this happens, a planet is in its **dignity.** But when it is in the sign opposite to the one(s) it rules, its influence is weaker than usual. This is sometimes referred to as a planet being in its **detriment**. Thus, when Saturn moves through Aquarius and Capricorn, it is in its dignity and particularly powerful. But when it moves through the signs directly across from those it rules, in this case Leo and Cancer, it is in its detriment and its influence is far less.

Planets that govern opposite signs to one another are said to be "enemies." For instance, Saturn (ruler of Aquarius) would be enemies with the Sun (ruler of Leo). Planets that are enemies can be unfavorable when acting in conjunction.

THE CELESTIAL HOUSES

A bove your head is an imaginary circle that slices the Earth in half from the north to south pole. This is called the **Prime Vertical.** For astrological purposes this imaginary circle is divided into twelve equal divisions called **Houses,** six of which are above the horizon and six below it. The First House is the segment of the circle just below the Eastern horizon line (see the inner circle of the illustration on the following page). The rest of the Houses are then numbered in order in a counterclockwise direction.

There are four **angular** or **cardinal** Houses—the First, Fourth, Seventh, and Tenth House. These are the Houses where the angles of the chart (the

Ascendant, Midheaven, Imum Coeli, and Descendant) are located.

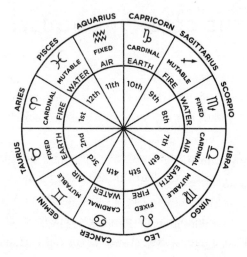

Each House has a meaning that has been established for centuries:

The First House governs personal appearance, specifically the face and head.

The Second House rules over finance, material possessions, commerce, and work. In the body it governs the neck and throat.

The Third House governs short journeys, communication, family, and neighbors. In the body it governs the arms and lungs.

The Fourth House governs real estate, the home, plants, mothers and motherhood, and the end of life. In the body, the breasts and thorax.

The Fifth House rules over children, sex, romantic relationships, and social pleasures. In the body, the back and heart.

The Sixth House governs the health, personal comforts, clothes, food and other necessities, sanitation, and hygiene. In the body it rules over the abdomen and lower organs.

The Seventh House has dominion over marriage, contracts, agreements, partners, and business relationships. In the body it is related to the reproductive organs and kidneys.

The Eighth House rules death, loss, inheritances, and matters relating to the deceased. In the body it is related to the excretory system.

The Ninth House is said to govern long journeys, writing and books, religious beliefs,

foreign lands, and legal affairs. In the body it
rules the thighs.

The Tenth House rules over position and reputation, honor and fame, the father, and authority figures. In the body it rules over the
knees.

The Eleventh House governs friends, social
groups, and clubs or companies the subject
is associated with. In the body it is related to
the legs from calf to ankle.

The Twelfth House rules ambushes, restraints,
difficulties, imprisonment, confinement, and
all limitations of personal freedom. In the
body it rules the ankles and feet.

If we apply these meanings to the interpretation
of a horoscope you'll notice, for instance, that if Mars
is rising at the moment of birth—meaning it is positioned at the starting edge of the First House—there
will be a scar or mark on the face because the First
House is connected with the face and head. These
sorts of observations can help determine the time of
someone's birth if it is unknown.

If a House falls under a particular sign, it can be

said that the planet that rules over that sign is also the ruler of that House, since it has fallen within its domain in the context of the reading. Thus, if we read a chart where the Fifth House is located in Cancer— which is ruled by the Moon—we could also say that the Moon is ruling over the Fifth House.

THE ASTRONOMICAL
ASPECTS

Aspects are the angular distances between the planets as they move around the wheel of the zodiac, and they are a fundamental part of astrology. Any planet may be good or bad in its effects on the subject, depending on the aspect that it throws to the main points of the horoscope. There are six aspects:

Semisquare	45 degrees	Evil/Negative
Sextile	60 degrees	Good/Positive
Square	90 degrees	Evil/Negative
Trine	120 degrees	Good/Positive
Sesquiquadrate	135 degrees	Evil/Negative
Opposition	180 degrees	Evil/Negative

In addition to those six, there is also **conjunction**, which describes when two planets are separated by less than one degree.

The good aspects, which are positive and auspicious, are trine and sextile; the evil aspects, which involve more difficulty and struggle, are the semisquare, square, sesquiquadrate, and opposition. The aspect of a planet determines its effects, whether positive or negative. Conjunction will depend on the planets involved; it is good with good planets, such as Jupiter and Venus, and evil with malefic planets such as Mars and Saturn.

When planets are the same distance North or South of the Equator they are in **parallel declination**, and they then act as if in conjunction. Also, when planets are in **mutual disposition**, that is to say, occupying one another's signs, they act as if they were in conjunction.

Planets in conjunction act according to their simple natures (see page 119), but when they are in aspect, they act according to the nature of that aspect, regardless of their own nature. The **benefic planets**, Jupiter, Venus, Sun, Moon, and also Mercury when in good disposition with another planet or in a congenial sign, produce good effects by their conjunctions and by their trine and sextile aspects; but when in square, semisquare, or sesquiquadrate aspect they have a negative effect. On the other hand, the **malefic planets** Neptune, Uranus, Saturn, and Mars, together with Mercury when ill-disposed or in uncongenial signs, are evil in their effects when in conjunction with the significant points of the horoscope or when they are in evil aspect. But their own natures notwithstanding, they produce positive effects when in good aspect.

The Significators

Significators are key indicators in the horoscope. The typical significators in any horoscope are the Sun, the Moon, the **Midheaven** (which is the highest point on a chart, indicating the degree which holds the meridian of the horoscope), and the Ascendant (the degree which is rising). But every planet can be a particular significator in its own province, that is when it's in the sign which it rules or in the house in which it was found during the subject's birth.

In a general sense the Moon is significant of the mother, female relationships, personal health and fortune, and all things related to these things. Similarly, the Sun indicates the father, male relationships, the vital principle, and status. Mercury is the significator of the mind and intellect, and the senses in general.

Venus is significator of love affairs, domestic relations, pleasure, and of young female relationships, sisters, etc. Mars is significator of enterprises, conflict, and young male relations. Jupiter is significator of wealth and profit; Saturn of inheritances and elderly people; Uranus of civic and governmental bodies; Neptune of journeys and psychic experiences. However, the most important points to consider are the Midheaven, the Ascendant, and the places of the Sun and Moon.

HOW TO READ A HOROSCOPE

CREATING YOUR
STAR CHART

To begin reading a horoscope, you'll first need a natal chart or star chart for the subject of the reading. This chart shows the location of the planets and luminaries at the time of the subject's birth. Refer to the resources section at the end of the book for a list of online resources where you can easily download your star chart for free.

THE PLANETS IN THE
HOUSES

In order to understand the effects of a planet in a horoscope, one must consider three things: The House they are located in, the sign they are located in, and the aspects they have with other planets. It's impossible to define the effects of just one of these factors apart from the rest.

Once you have digested the nature of the planets, and the dominion of the Houses, it's simple to judge the effects they might have. So the first step in reading a horoscope is to consider in which House a planet is located. Then you can evaluate the nature of the planet according to the following chart:

Neptune means chaos, confusion, and deception.

Uranus means eccentricity, originality, and estrangement.

Saturn means lack, obstacles, and denial.

Jupiter means affluence, fruitfulness, and increase.

Sun means recognition and honor.

Mars means excess, impulse, and quarreling.

Venus means peace, happiness, and agreement.

Mercury means commerce, versatility, and adaptability.

Moon means changes and attention.

After that, consider what aspects of life are governed by the House in which the planet is located (page 27).

For instance, suppose Saturn is found in the Eleventh House. Saturn is "lack" and the Eleventh House is the domain of friends. So we can interpret this as a lack of friendship for the subject. Jupiter in the Second House, in the same manner, would signify increase of money and possessions. Mars in the Seventh House would indicate quarrels with partners or in the context of a business relationship. Each planet reflects its own nature on the elements of life governed by the House in which it is found at the moment of birth.

Not infrequently, there will be more than one planet in the same House. Let's suppose that two planets occupy the same House. In such case one may be good (Jupiter), and the other malefic (Mars). In that instance, first consider the planet that is in the earlier part of the House—the one closer to the horizon or the Midheaven—and then the second planet. Thus, Saturn followed by Jupiter in the Eleventh House would signify trouble from friends or advisors in the first part of life (Saturn), followed by some good fortune from the same source in the second part of the subject's life. The degrees between the planets will indicate the years which elapse between these changes of fortune. The same process applies if there are more than two planets in the same House. In those cases, you can safely predict that the person will experience a great deal of change in the area of their life ruled by that House.

However, a planet being located in a House is not the whole story or a sufficient basis for interpretation. You must also account for the third element: the aspects of the planet. If Saturn is in good aspect to any of the significators—the Sun, Moon, Ascendant, or Midheaven—and well aspected by other planets, it is a more positive sign than Jupiter when it is badly placed and in poor aspect. Jupiter has his own ill effects, and Saturn has his good influences. Jupiter is only a benefic when acting by conjunction or good aspect with another planet, and Saturn is only a malefic when acting by conjunction or evil aspect.

Once you have considered all of these elements—the nature of the planet, the House it is positioned in, and its aspect—with a little practice you'll soon find you can easily read a horoscope.

THE CONSTITUTION

The Sun is the chief significator of the constitution, so the aspects it has to other planets are important. If the Sun is in good aspect, or at least not in evil aspect, to the other planets, then the physical condition of the subject is likely to be good.

However, if the Sun is afflicted by some planets and assisted by others, the subject will have an average constitution, and you will have to judge whether the influence of the other planets is predominately positive or negative. When the afflicting planets are angular—that is to say, in the First, Fourth, Seventh, or Tenth Houses (see page 27)—the congenital or hereditary tendency to disease is made stronger. But when the assisting planets are angular, the predisposition to disease is far less.

The likelihood of illness can be evaluated based on the evil aspects relative to the Sun. We can determine which part of the body will be affected by considering which sign the afflicting planets are located in.

On page 14, we cited the various illnesses associated with the planets. But the signs are also grouped together based on their effects on health.

The Movable Signs—Aries, Cancer, Libra, and Capricorn—are related to the head, stomach, skin, kidneys, liver, and spine.

The Fixed Signs—Taurus, Leo, Scorpio, and Aquarius—are related to the throat, heart, blood, and excretory system.

The Mutable Signs—Gemini, Virgo, Sagittarius, and Pisces—are related to the lungs, bowels, and nervous system.

When the Sun is afflicted by several planets, and there is no assistance from the good aspects or conjunctions of other bodies, then the subject will likely suffer from weak health and possibly an early death.

But when there are several planets afflicting and at the same time some benefic influences from others, it's more common to see some disease and physical weakness but a long life.

Death in infancy often occurs when the malefic planets are immediately rising or culminating in evil aspect while the luminaries (Sun and Moon) are located below the horizon. Or when there are malefic planets immediately setting or passing the nadir (the bottom of the chart, opposite the Midheaven), in evil aspect to the luminaries below the horizon. But when there are mitigating influences from the good aspects of the benefic planets, or the luminaries, the person will live, though perhaps will struggle with their health.

HEALTH AND SICKNESS

The aspects of the Moon are the primary factors when considering sickness. If the Moon is in evil aspect with several planets with no relief from being in good aspect with other planets, then the subject's health will be fragile with frequent illness. However, if the Moon is generally in good aspect to the other planets, the person will experience good health and be generally unaffected by sickness.

This interpretation is similar to the Sun's impact on a person's constitution, which we explored in the previous chapter, except in this instance we've simply substituted the Moon for the Sun. While the Sun governs the vital power, the Moon governs the functional powers, and while the Sun is related to conditions that are congenital or hereditary, the Moon is related to illness or physical conditions that occur after birth. Similarly, the Sun is related to factors which are incidental to the body, while the Moon denotes factors that are accidental to the body.

SUN	MOON
Organic	Functional
Hereditary	Acquired
Incidental	Accidental

You will notice that while someone's constitution (related to the Sun) may be strong, their health (related to the Moon) can be very bad at times. On the other hand, the health may be good, while a person's constitution is weak. In the first case, the person would experience a long life, but one that involved frequent sickness; in the second case the person would enjoy a life that is relatively free of sickness only to be bowled over by the first serious illness they experience due to their weak constitution.

Only when the Sun and Moon are both unafflicted by evil aspects or conjunctions, meaning both the health and constitution are good, can we be confident that there is every indication of a robust and vigorous life reaching a ripe old age.

When the Sun and Moon are both in negative aspect, and there is no relief from any good aspects, it is likely that the person in question will die very young.

Because of the connections between constitution and health, if the Moon is in good aspect to the Sun at birth it is an excellent sign, indicating harmony between the organic and the functional. When this alignment happens, the subject will find that they recover remarkably well and are quickly back to health even after serious sickness.

Malefic planets rising and afflicting either the Sun or Moon indicate prolonged ill health, and most frequently some permanent hurt to the body.

If a rising planet (the planet nearest to the Eastern horizon) is malefic and in negative aspect with either the Sun or Moon, it can indicate prolonged periods of illness or permanent damage to the body.

If a horoscope reveals that the subject will be predisposed to illness, the type of illness can be determined by the sign in which the afflicting planet is located. Thus, if Saturn is in Aries and in negative aspect with the Moon, you can expect some kind of head injury (Aries) along with chills and colds, influenza, a runny nose, etc. (Saturn). Similarly, Mars in Leo would indicate functional defects of the heart (Leo) due to accelerated action and overstrain, such as result from fevers (Mars).

A good aspect of the planets Jupiter and Venus is helpful in counteracting the influence of malefic aspects or evil positions.

HOW TO READ CHARACTER
AND DISPOSITION

Ptolemy says: "Mercury is the ruler of the rational soul, the Moon of the animal soul." By this he means that Mercury is related to the rational, thinking mind, while the Moon is related to biological brain function. There are certain attributes of the mind which are distinctive to human beings, while other aspects are found in both people and animals. The latter are under the dominion of the Moon, while Mercury has chief signification of the rational mind and mental faculties.

Thus, when considering the frame of mind and disposition of a person, we look at the position and aspects of Mercury on their chart. They are the mental significators.

Planets that are in conjunction or aspect to either the Moon or Mercury will impart their nature strongly on the subject's character and disposition. We've already discussed the natures of the planets (pages 40–41), so we now only need to consider the type of aspect that is thrown to the mental significators by the other bodies. For instance, the Sun being in trine to the Moon will create independence and dignity, while the square aspect or opposition of the Sun would indicate an excess of pride that will hinder the subject's relationships. In the same way, the good aspect of Jupiter indicates benevolence and regulated philanthropy, while the opposition or other evil aspect of the same planet would indicate extravagance and ostentatious displays of charity.

The good and bad aspects of the planets can be summed up as:

PLANETS	IN GOOD ASPECT	IN EVIL ASPECT
Neptune	genius, inspiration	insanity, obsession
Uranus	originality, invention	stubborness, eccentricity

Saturn	steadfastness, fidelity	deceitfulness, suspicion
Jupiter	benevolence, joviality	ostentation, extravagance
Mars	energy, decisiveness	impulsivity, destructiveness
Sun	dignity, independence	vanity, egotism
Venus	affability, artfulness	self-indulgence, disorderliness
Mercury	alertness, ingenuity	inquisitiveness, meddling
Moon	grace, idealism	inconstancy, awkwardness

The overall disposition and frame of mind of the subject is indicated by the position of the majority of the planets according to the constitution of the signs they occupy. So, if the majority of the planets are found in:

The Cardinal Signs it indicates executive ability, business aptitude, a pioneer spirit, ambition, and capability to create a place for oneself and to make headway against obstacles. Such people are usually at the forefront in their particular sphere of life, and are always found in the most progressive movements, re-forms, etc.

The Fixed Signs it indicates stability, patience, endurance, method, caution, and diplomacy. Such people are likely to become the originators of schools of thought, policies, and schemes. They have a settled purpose, determination, independence, and pivotal stability. They sit still and the world revolves around them.

The Mutable Signs it indicates versatility, flexibility, suavity, adaptability, and lack of originality. Such people usually have too many irons in the fire, and often bite off more than they can chew. This is due to their versatility. They have a superficial knowledge of many things, but lack the persistence to bring that knowledge to practical effect. At the same time their adaptability leads to many successes in life, and their agreeableness, sympathy, and charm create many friends for them.

In the Wheel of Life, the cardinal signs denote the outer rim which is ever on the move, and experiences the greatest acceleration. The mutable signs are the spokes of the wheel, uniting the rim to the hub, and in that sense representing the power of adaptability.

The fixed signs represent the hub, which remains quiescent and still, which is useful in its stability and lack of movement.

While the sign-groupings of the planets are useful in giving the keynote of the subject's nature and disposition, the particular details of the subject's disposition can only be judged by considering the aspects of the planets to the Moon and Mercury. In addition, planets that occupy the Third and Ninth House—which are related to the mind and its expression—along with any planet that is rising at the moment of birth will also strongly impact the subject's nature, regardless of how these planets are aspected to the mental rulers.

It's important to pay attention to the position and aspects of the planets that are in aspect to the mental rulers, because if they are badly placed, in oppositional signs, or are badly aspected by other planets, they will not have the same impact and force as they otherwise would.

Of course, in all astrological analysis, we must admit that the effects of genetics, upbringing, and association play a role. A man who came from a difficult family situation, suffered malnourishment, and never attended school will have a different disposition than someone who hasn't experienced those situations—no matter how favorable his aspects may be. I have no doubt that many a clodpole was born under similar aspects to those of Shakespeare, Raphael, Newton, or Cæsar. I am not dismayed. *Non gli astri muovono solamente per Roma!* There must be countless geniuses who never received the conditions they needed to thrive and amaze the world.

But to continue. The inspirational and passionate temperament is indicated by the majority of planets being in fiery signs. The mental or intellectual temperament is shown by the majority appearing in aerial signs, the psychic or emotional temperament by the majority in watery signs, and the practical or indulgent temperament by the majority being in earthy signs.

The subject's rising sign often has a strong impact on their personality. The characteristics of the rising sign are determined by the planet that governs it and the "elemental" nature of the sign itself. Thus, if Cancer is a person's rising sign, they would be impacted by the characteristics of the Moon and by the temperament associated with water signs.

All of this information gives you the key to an individual's character, and you'll soon see from experience how accurate it can be.

Disorders

When either the Moon or Mercury is afflicted by the malefic planets, and there are no relieving aspects from the benefic planets—Jupiter, Venus, or the Sun—the subject is likely to be predisposed to brain and nervous system disorders. This is more of a concern when the Moon or Mercury is afflicted in the mutable signs. This observation has been scientifically established by Mr. A. G. Trent, in his little work entitled "The Soul and the Stars," which is an excellent reference if you would like to learn more.

FINANCES

To learn about a person's financial outlook, we look to the planets that are located in the Second House, and the aspects to them. If the planets in the Second House are well aspected, the subject's financial prospects will be solid. If a benefic (Jupiter or Venus) is located in the Second House, and free from evil aspects, the same will be true. Even better, if the benefic in the Second has good aspects from other planets, then the subject will enjoy considerable wealth.

For instance, Mars in the Second House, well aspected, reflects good earning capacity, because Mars is an ambitious and industrious planet (i.e., it produces such effects in the person), and the Second House is the domain of finance. But at the same time, if badly aspected, it indicates extravagance and inability to save money, because Mars is impulsive and lacking thrift.

Any planet in the Second House, badly aspected, will produce difficulty in earning money, and if a malefic planet occupies the Second House under these conditions, there will be times of stress and even poverty.

If the chart shows a malefic planet in the Second House in evil aspect to the Moon or Sun while, at the same time, the other planets in the Second House are in negative aspect, this is a very grim foretelling. The person's life will be marked by continual hardship and poverty.

Saturn in the Midheaven in negative aspect to the Sun or Moon indicates a reversal of fortune. People with this combination in their chart often rise to a high position in their life only to end up losing everything.

Jupiter or Venus in the Tenth House, and near the meridian, are signs of good fortune and success in life. The same is true if they are rising at birth.

The planets that are in good aspect to the Moon (in a male horoscope) and the Sun (in a female horoscope) will reflect the means by which the subject will gain their wealth. Similarly, planets in evil aspect to the Moon and Sun will suggest sources of financial loss based on which House the afflicting planet is located in.

Thus Jupiter in good aspect to the Moon from the Eleventh House shows financial gain through friends, advisers, and cooperative measures, because the Eleventh House rules these relationships and Jupiter is the index of increase. Similarly, Uranus in the Seventh House would indicate gain via marriage if in good aspect to the Moon, or loss in the same way if it is in evil aspect.

The Sixth House well occupied shows faithful employees who will do good work and increase the fortune of the subject.

Neptune in the Second shows complications and involved finances, and often loss by fraud; though in good aspect to other planets it reflects gain by such nefarious means. Uranus indicates many ups and downs of fortune, sudden and unexpected rises and falls.

Thus each planet is judged based on its own nature and the aspect it throws to the Moon or Sun, while the planets in the Second House are judged by their own natures and the aspects which they receive.

Inheritance is shown by a benefic planet in the Fifth or Eleventh House in good aspect to Saturn; but indirect inheritance can be the result of Saturn in good aspect to Jupiter from any part of the chart.

Legacies are shown by good planets, or planets well aspected, in the Eighth House; or by Jupiter in good aspect to Uranus from any part of the heavens.

Gain by marriage is shown by benefic planets in the Eighth House, because the Eighth is Second from the Seventh, and the Seventh House rules over the partner.

The positive aspects of each horoscope can be increased by paying attention to the sources of gain as they are indicated by the position and aspects of the planets. However, the primary way to build on the positive aspects of a chart is by associating with someone whose own horoscope works in harmony with your own. Individuals can be lifted to high positions and affluence through their associations with sympathetic horoscopes (see "Friends and Enemies," page 87, for more information).

The Sun and Moon being in good aspect to one another will prevent disaster, or will always provide a way of restoring prosperity, because this indicates continual support and general good fortune. People who have this aspect in their horoscopes don't ever need to fear misfortune. If disaster strikes, they will always come out on top. But when the Sun and Moon are in evil aspect, and particularly when the malefic planets are in elevation in the heavens, the subject will experience continual misfortune. Even if there are periods of good fortune, they will be short.

If the benefic planets, Jupiter, Venus, and the Sun, are well elevated in the heavens (in the Tenth or Eleventh Houses), it is a sign of exceedingly good fortune. But when the malefics are in elevation the reverse is true.

STATUS

I n general, a subject's status and position in the
world are determined by the position of the majority of the planets, but more specifically by the Midheaven, the planets located there, and its aspects. For
instance, if you find the majority of the planets rising
(that is, located in the Tenth, Eleventh, Twelfth, First,
Second, and Third Houses) the subject will be a can-
didate for responsibility, highly ambitious, and generally independent. If these planets, or the majority
of them, are well aspected they will become a person of
influence, commanding the respect and attention
of others in either the business or social sphere.

If Midheaven is in good aspect from the major

planets, the subject will enjoy a secure and honorable position in life.

If Venus, Jupiter, or the Sun is well aspected to the Midheaven, this is particularly auspicious and indicates that the subject will rise to a high status of particular distinction. The same is true if these three are rising.

When the majority of the planets are above the horizon (in Houses Seven through Twelve), even if they are not rising, the subject will find themselves charged with responsibilities, even though they do not particularly desire them. If the majority of these planets are well aspected, the subject will rise to the occasion and be rewarded for their work.

When evaluating a chart to determine someone's status and position, it's always fortunate if there are planets exactly on the cusps of the Second, Third, Sixth, Eighth, or Twelfth Houses. This indicates that they will enjoy fame and advancement in life.

However, if any of the malefic planets are found exactly on or nearest to the meridian, whether above or below the horizon, the subject will experience a fall from grace, loss of position, poor reputation, or disgrace.

The Tenth House represents fame and honor, and the Fourth House represents the end of life and the forces that prevent fame and honor. Therefore, when there are good planets in these places, the subject will meet with rewards and honors for their work; but when evil planets occupy the meridian, they will struggle to maintain their position.

Tempting as it may be to believe, a benefic planet located in the meridian of your horoscope does not mean that you will achieve fame and fortune without effort. The planets influence human affairs via human thought and action, and through fixed laws, never by chance. The old wisdom that "the Gods help those who help themselves" is a truth that astrology supports.

A large proportion of planets placed in cardinal signs will create a desire to seek fame, and when the Midheaven of the horoscope is well aspected or if there are fortunate planets located there, the subject will attain it. Cardinal signs on the angles of the horoscope (the meridian and horizon), indicate a fame that will outlast death. The same is true if either of the luminaries are exactly on the equinoxes. But if the luminaries are heavily afflicted the subject will experience ups and downs in life, gaining and losing status repeatedly throughout their life.

If Venus is located in the Midheaven it indicates social elevation and lifts a person above the sphere of birth. Good planets in the Eleventh House show patronage.

If the majority of the planets are under the horizon, this shows success in the latter part of life, while if they are between the Fourth and Seventh cusps, there will be advancement after marriage or through a partner.

In order to judge how the subject will sustain their position in life, we must consider the nature of the planets that are in good aspect to the Midheaven or which benefic planets are in the Midheaven. If there are none, then consider the nature and sign of any planets in good aspect to the Sun and Moon, giving preference to the planet that has the strongest positive aspect. Thus, if two planets were in trine (a good aspect) the one with the higher elevation would be the one to focus on, particularly if it was also in good aspect to other planets.

OCCUPATION

Knowing their own aptitude would save countless young people a great deal of time and effort as they decide on which career path to pursue. The average person can't make up their mind about what they would like to do for work because they do not know enough about their own capabilities or about what a job will require. Parents have the same problem. They have to wait and see how their child grows up, paying attention to her inclinations as much as they can, but without any definite conclusion as to what type of career would be best. After getting a solid education—one that would in theory prepare her for anything, but that doesn't give her any specialized knowledge—she's dropped at a desk in an office and left to her own devices. With luck, she may find herself suited to her work. More frequently she spends several years realizing that she has missed her calling entirely, that she has wasted her time and made a false start in a career that holds no interest for her. Or perhaps a student was fortunate to come from a well-off background and enjoyed the benefits of elite higher education—after paying a small fortune for the privilege. But then he discovers that he is really an actor meant for the theater, and the law degree he earned is nothing but a waste. If nothing else, astrology can save everyone a great deal of time and money by skipping this entire situation.

It's a law of nature that the line of least resistance is the path of greatest progress. The lightning flash doesn't come straight to Earth, but zigzags down, following the line of least resistance. Rivers don't flow directly to the ocean, but make their way with many turns and twists, because they follow the easiest path. If you think about the years people spend hammering away in jobs and professions that aren't a good fit, it's wise to remember the rule of nature. Choose the path that will allow you to make the greatest progress instead of battling your own nature every day. And here too the stars can offer guidance.

The career path and inclinations of the subject are judged based on the position of the majority of the planets. If the majority of the planets are found in the aerial signs—Gemini, Libra, or Aquarius—the subject will have an inclination towards mental and intellectual occupations, especially science and literature. If the majority are located in the fiery signs, Aries, Leo, and Sagittarius, there is a predisposition to a more robust and active type of job, perhaps military service, forestry, field work, etc. If the majority reside in the earthy signs, Taurus, Virgo, and Capricorn, the aptitude lies in the direction of agriculture, experimental science, surveying, real estate, etc. If the watery signs, Cancer, Scorpio, and Pisces, hold the majority, there is special inclination to pursuits connected with the water, such as joining the navy, marine biology, sanitation, etc.; but also to other occupation in which liquid features prominently, such as sommeliers, chemists, or fluid engineering.

Each sign has its own unique tendency, and the

subject's exact occupation can often be illuminated when we consider the planet that has a trine or sextile aspect of the Moon and is elevated above the malefic planets. If this planet is also in good aspect to the other planets, it is particularly important. The House this planet is located in will indicate the type of work the subject is best suited for, while the sign it is in will indicate the means by which the money will arrive.

Aries denotes soldiers and entrepreneurs; Taurus shows dealers in real estate, house agents and brokers; Gemini, literary people and writers of all sorts; Cancer, sailors and restaurateurs; Leo, actors and artists; Virgo, those involved in fashion as well as bakers; Libra, appraisers, bankers, and pawnbrokers; Scorpio, naval sailors, chemists, purveyors of wine and spirits; Sagittarius, forest rangers, spiritual guides, lawyers; Capricorn, political agents and civil servants; Aquarius, electricians, marketers, and scientific researchers; Pisces, fishmongers, caretakers, and those connected with places of confinement, such as prisons and hospitals.

Considering both the sign of the dominant planet and the signs that hold the majority of the planets in the chart, we can easily see someone's most natural and successful career path.

No one will make a good soldier if Mars is not the dominant planet nor will they become a successful artist, musician, or poet if Venus is not well placed in the horoscope.

Generally, the direction of the subject's career path is, as we have discussed, derived by considering the dominant planet, and the measure of success that the subject will enjoy in that occupation is judged from the aspect that planet has toward the Sun or the Moon. There's nothing to be gained by pursuing a career that will ultimately prove unsuccessful, which is exactly what will happen if the dominant planet is in bad aspect to the luminaries. And yet, good work has never been done without the motivation of strong inclination and enthusiasm. So in some instances, the subject will find that they must pursue their passion even if their success is not predicted. The pursuit of passion may involve sacrificing some of the benefits of life. "Take what thou wilt, but pay the price!" is, according to Emerson, the Divine mandate.

But without a doubt the science of astrology, which

enables a person to choose the line of least resistance and prevents them from wasting years of their life pursuing the wrong career, is worth a little study. "Hitch your wagon to a star" is good advice if we hitch it to the right one.

LOVE AND MARRIAGE

The question of how, when, and where you will fall in love is an all-consuming one for many people, and it is a both an important and interesting question. Astrology has made it possible for us to answer these questions of the heart accurately and precisely.

Matters of love and marriage are judged by the relationship between the Moon and Venus (indicative of a partner with female energy) and from the relationship between the Sun and Mars (indicative of a partner with masculine energy). The first planet that the luminary, whether sun or moon, forms an aspect with after birth (the first it "applies" to) indicates the subject's partner. If the aspect is good, the relationship will thrive, but if the aspect is negative there will be trouble. The nature of the planet in aspect to the luminary is also significant. If the luminary is in good aspect to a benefic planet, or to one that is well-placed and aspected, then the relationship will thrive. On the other hand, if both the aspect and the planet are evil—for instance if the Moon was found to be in opposition to Saturn or Uranus or Mars—then the relationship will be extremely rocky, with frequent and perhaps permanent disagreements.

When the aspect and nature of the planet are mixed—such as if the Moon was in good aspect to Saturn or in bad aspect to Jupiter—the subject's love life will experience both good and bad. There is no better sign of happiness and harmony in marriage than a good aspect between the Sun and Moon.

It may happen that the Moon is in good aspect to a planet after birth, but that there is also a malefic body in the Seventh House (the House which symbolizes relationships and marriage). This indicates that there will be happiness and love, but that grief will soon follow.

When the Moon applies to Neptune there will be some peculiarity or touch of genius in the partner, depending on how Neptune is aspected. Uranus shows eccentricity and sometimes willfulness. Saturn indicates steadiness, industry; or jealousy and coldness. Jupiter indicates a good nature, bountiful and honest, but perhaps inclined to excess and extravagance. Mars induces industry and practicality, but it also brings a strong temper and a tendency to be a loner. The Sun shows dignity and loyalty, but may indicate ostentation and foolish pride. Venus denotes peacefulness and a genial, classy nature, but in the negative it brings indifference, neglect, and disorderliness. Mercury denotes an active and energetic nature, but may produce a busybody and meddler.

Everything depends on the aspect the significant luminary throws to the planet it applies to. If the aspect is good it will indicate the better qualities of that planet; but if it's evil, the subject's partner will often exhibit the negative qualities of the planet in question.

Marriage to a widow or widower occurs when Mars and Saturn are the planets at play, for instance if Mars is in the Seventh House and in aspect to Saturn, or if the Moon applies to Mars when aspected by Saturn, or when one of them is in the Fifth House and the other in the Seventh.

Love affairs before marriage are indicated by the Fifth House, the planets therein and their aspects, and in a general sense by Venus (for feminine energy) and Mars (for masculine energy).

Thus if Venus (or Mars) is in negative aspect with Saturn or Uranus there will be disappointment in the early affections. Uranus in aspect to Venus/Mars gives romantic attachments and indicates a powerful influence over potential partners. Neptune in aspect shows idealism, and when afflicting Venus/Mars it produces chaos and entanglement, danger of seduction.

More Than One Marriage

There are several ways that multiple marriages or serious relationships can be read in the chart. Multiple romantic entanglements are indicated when the luminary is in aspect to more than one planet in a double-bodied sign (Gemini, Sagittarius, or Pisces). Or, if the luminary itself is in a double sign and in aspect to any planet other than one in the Seventh House. A double sign on the cusp of the Seventh House combined with the luminary in a fruitful sign (Cancer, Scorpio, or Pisces), or in aspect to planets in those signs, also indicates multiple marriages.

Likewise, there are several indicators of divorce or separation. The luminary applying to the ill aspect of a malefic planet, Venus afflicted, and Uranus in the Seventh House or afflicting the Moon or Venus, all indicate separation or divorce. For subjects whose partners display masculine energy, consider the Sun and Mars instead of the Moon and Venus, and evaluate the same indicators.

If more than one marriage is indicated, the ruler of the Seventh House indicates the first partner (see pages 28–30 to determine the ruler of a house). The planet ruling the sign it occupies is called its "dispositor" or "displacer." This dispositor represents the second partner.

The planet to which the significant luminary applies describes the partner, according to the sign it is in. But if this planet is in retrograde, i.e., going backwards in the zodiac by apparent motion, then it only represents a fleeting attachment that will be broken off. Its dispositor then becomes the significator of the partner. But the ruler of the Seventh House indicates the condition and fortunes of the partner, and if it is afflicted or badly placed in the horoscope, then the marriage or relationship will be unsatisfying and contentious. The opposite is the case if the significant planet is well placed and aspected.

We can determine the place and circumstances under which the subject will meet their partner by the sign and house occupied by the planet to which the luminary first applies after birth. Thus, if it's in the Eleventh House, the partner will be met among friends, at the home of a friend, or introduced by a friend. In the Third House, they will meet on a short trip or via letter or messages; in the Fifth, at a place of entertainment; in the Tenth, in the course of business; and so on.

CHILDREN

The Fifth House, the planets located within it, and the position and aspects of the Moon all must be considered when evaluating the subject's family life.

If the Fifth House is occupied by benefic planets, or planets that are well aspected, then the subject's children will be a source of pride and joy. But the opposite is the case if the Fifth House is occupied by malefic planets or planets that are in negative aspect.

The Moon represents the tendency in the male and the capacity in the female, and when well aspected, or free from evil aspects and well placed, then there will be good fortune for the subject's family and children.

When Uranus afflicts a planet in the Fifth House,

there will be some premature births. In general if planets are opposed from the Eleventh and Fifth Houses, or malefic planets occupy those Houses, there will be trouble or loss in the family.

There is no exact way to determine the number of children a subject will have. However, the nature of the sign on the cusp of the Fifth House is usually used as an approximation. Aries, Leo, and Capricorn tend to indicate small families. Taurus, Cancer, Virgo, Scorpio, and Pisces suggest large families, and the other signs hint at an average-sized family. When the Moon is strong, angular, and not afflicted, more children are suggested. Twins are born when double-bodied signs are occupying the cusp of the Fifth House, or when planets in the Fifth House are in a double-bodied sign.

The nature of each child is evaluated from alternate Houses, beginning with the Fifth. Thus, the first child (in a male horoscope) is ruled by the Fifth House, and planets therein; the second child by the Seventh House; the third by the Ninth House, and so on. In a female horoscope the first child is ruled by the Fourth House; the second by the Sixth House, and so on.

If the chart indicates sickness or ill health for any

of the children, the child whose House contains malefic planets or those in bad aspect is likely to be the
one to suffer.

Successful children are born to the subject when
the ruler of the Fifth House is in elevation and well
aspected, and in a congenial sign. But if the ruler of
the Fifth House is badly placed and aspected and in a
sign of debility (opposite to one over which it rules),
then the children will likely struggle in life. More details about the lives of the children can be found by
reading their own individual charts.

When malefic planets hold the Twelfth House in a
female horoscope, there will be risk during childbirth;
the same happens if either of the luminaries, but particularly the Moon, are afflicted in the Fifth House.

TRAVEL

Travel can be judged based on the Third House and the planets found within it. If a movable sign (Aries, Cancer, Libra, and Capricorn) is on the cusp of the Third House, or planets in a movable sign occupy the Third House, then the subject will travel frequently and there will be many short trips to and fro. The aspects to these planets in the Third will indicate whether such journeys will be successful or not. When there are no aspects to the planet or planets in the Third House we can judge the success of these travels by simply considering the nature of the planet in the Third. For instance, Jupiter would indicate fortunate and lucrative trips; but Saturn would indicate

travel plagued by delays and difficulties. When malefic planets are afflicted in the Third House, or malefic planets in the Third throw evil aspects to the Sun
or Moon, the Subject will encounter danger and accidents in their travels.

Watery signs on the cusp of the Third House, or
planets in watery signs in the Third, indicate cruising
and yachting, and short journeys by water around the
coast. If the Moon is in good aspect to these planets,
then these journeys will be safe; but if it is afflicted by
the planets in the Third there will be danger of col-
lision, capsizing, etc. according to the nature of the
planet in the Third House.

Long voyages and trips can be judged in exactly
the same manner based on the Ninth House, the
planets located there and their aspects.

The Fourth House indicates the place of birth. If
this House has a benefic planet, or either the Sun or
Moon, well aspected, then the subject will experience
good fortune in their hometown and should only
venture further afield when the journey is also indicated to be fortunate and will allow them to return
home. When, however, the Fourth House is occupied

by evil planets or planets heavily afflicted, it's advisable that the subject move from their hometown and build their life in a more fortunate location.

The choice of where to relocate can be guided by the planet that holds the greatest power for good in the horoscope. The quarter of the heavens that it occupies will indicate the direction the subject should consider.

The points of the compass follow the cardinal points of the heavens, the Midheaven being South; the Nadir, North; the Ascendant, East; and the Descendant, West. Thus, if the planet is between the East horizon and the meridian, the subject should move Southeast; between the meridian and the West horizon, Southwest; and so on. If a malefic planet is rising or setting at birth it is advisable for the subject to move their place of residence far enough East from their birthplace to bring the malefic planets out of the angles of the horoscope. The same is true if the malefic planets occupy the Tenth or Fourth Houses. On the contrary, if benefic planets are in the Third and Ninth Houses the subject should move Westward so as to bring the benefic influences into the Tenth and Fourth Houses.

When benefic planets or planets well aspected occupy the angles of the figure at birth the subject should not travel far or live far from their birthplace for an extended period of time.

A great deal of travel and voyages by sea are suggested if many of the planets are in watery signs (Cancer, Scorpio, and Pisces) and also in the sign Virgo. When the majority of the planets are in cardinal and mutable signs (Aries, Gemini, Cancer, Virgo, Libra, Sagittarius, Capricorn, and Pisces) there will be many changes and journeys. Also, if the Sun, Moon, Mars, and Mercury are in either the Third, Ninth, Twelfth, or Sixth Houses the subject will take many trips abroad and to foreign countries.

When planets are afflicted in watery signs the subject will experience danger at sea, and if the Moon or Sun are afflicted in Virgo they will experience a wreck, crash, or accident at sea.

If there are planets, especially malefics, in Scorpio, Leo, Taurus, and Aquarius, afflicted by the aspects of other planets, or themselves afflicting the Sun or Moon, there is danger of drowning.

When the signs of travel look fortunate, especially when the indications in the Fourth House are not so, it may be a good idea to leave your place of birth. But when good planets or planets well aspected are either rising or in the Fourth House, the subject should remain in their birth place because that location will prove beneficial.

FRIENDS AND ENEMIES

The general harmony of the horoscope is determined by the overall positions and aspects of the planets and their relations with the luminaries. When this is auspicious, the subject will enjoy many friends and supporters, and their associations will be pleasant and profitable. But when the horoscope is fraught with evil aspects and angular positions of the malefics, they will encounter a great deal of strife and conflict.

The friends and acquaintances of the subject can be evaluated more specifically by consulting the Eleventh House and the planets therein. If there be a benefic planet in the Eleventh, especially if in good aspect to either of the luminaries, the subject will enjoy many friends and positive relationships.

Similarly, the enemies of the subject can be evaluated by referencing the Seventh House. Secret enemies are determined by the Twelfth House. Malefic planets in either House, especially in evil aspect to the Sun or Moon, indicate that the subject will have to endure fierce adversaries.

Neptune in any malefic aspect to the Sun or Moon indicates a danger of deceit and treachery against the subject, and if this is combined with ill aspects from Mars or Uranus they will be in danger of violence or unexpected ambush. Saturn in the Seventh or Twelfth indicates long feuds and implacable enmities. Uranus in the same House indicates lawsuits and creditors. Mars reflects violence and passionate hatred. Mercury suggests scandal and continual petty annoyances.

Determining Friends and Enemies

Observe the places of the malefic planets and the Houses where they are situated. Take the date when the Sun is in the same longitude as any of these malefic planets, which will be the same in any year, and this will be the birthday of the people who will likely bring strife and conflict into the life of the subject. For instance suppose Saturn is found in the Tenth House, in the thirteenth degree of the sign Aquarius. Reference to an ephemeris[1] will show that the Sun is in Aquarius 13 on the first and second of February. Hence it would be unfortunate for the subject to work with anyone who was born between the twenty-eighth of January and the third of February in any year. Or if Uranus were in Leo 23 in the Seventh House he shouldn't enter a partnership or marriage with anybody born on or near the fifteenth of August in any year.

Now consider the places of the benefic planets as well as the place of the Moon, and find the corresponding solar dates. These will be the birthdays of people who will help and support the subject throughout their life.

The trines and sextiles of the benefic planets and of the Moon, and the squares and oppositions of the malefics, will operate in the same way, but in a more minor degree.

---

1 www.astro.com/swisseph/swepha_e.htm provides an excellent ephemeris for reference.

Comparing the horoscopes of people, whether they are kings or schoolteachers, with the horoscopes of the people who have been forces for good or evil in their lives will immediately confirm this method. There is nothing more dependable in the whole range of scientific observation than this sympathy and antipathy of horoscopes and their corresponding results. This is a strong argument in favor of those who claim that astrology should be considered a science. If the planets have no impact on the dispositions and tendencies of people, these patterns would not exist. If you find yourself unhappy in love compare your horoscopes and you will find your lover's chart does not align with your own. On the other hand, if you've ever been helped by a patron or mentor compare your horoscope with your benefactor and you'll see that the benefic planets in their chart hold the places of the Sun, Moon, Midheaven, or Ascendant in your own.

This often accounts for the fact that people with comparatively unfortunate horoscopes are sometimes found in positions of influence and enjoy good fortune. The complex fabric of life is woven from a rainbow of threads to complete the grand design. The loom of life moves in ways we cannot understand. We here below, as subjects of interplanetary action, must content ourselves with glimpsing the design as it is revealed to us in history, or we can seek to understand the purpose of life, its motif, the complex laws that operate to bring it about, and live our lives in light of what we discover.

DEATH

The end of life is judged based on the planets occupying the Eighth and Fourth Houses; the Eighth denotes death, and the Fourth denotes the final resting-place. When benefic planets, or the luminaries well aspected, occupy these Houses, the subject's death will be peaceful and unremarkable, and that death will take place in comfort surrounded by care.

When, however, the malefic planets hold these Houses, or afflict the luminaries therein, there will be greater stress or anxiety at the end of life.

Uranus in the Eighth House denotes a sudden death, and the same result occurs when the luminaries in the Eighth House are afflicted by Uranus.

Neptune in the Eighth denotes unconsciousness or coma. Saturn produces death by obstruction, cold, or hardship. Mars induces death by fevers and inflammation, and frequently by hemorrhage.

Planets in fixed signs (Taurus, Leo, Scorpio, and Aquarius) in the Eighth House indicate death related to the heart or throat, the excretory system and the blood. In cardinal signs (Aries, Cancer, Libra, Capricorn), the head, stomach, kidneys, or skin are the cause of the fatal disease. In mutable signs (Gemini, Virgo, Sagittarius, and Pisces), the lungs, bowels, and nervous system become fatally affected.

Violent or unnatural deaths are indicated when either of the luminaries is simultaneously afflicted by the evil aspects of more than one of the malefic planets, or when both luminaries are separately afflicted by the evil aspects of malefic planets.

In these situations, Neptune produces death by assassination; Uranus by sudden catastrophe, explosions, electricity, and machinery; Saturn by blows and falling; and Mars by cuts, burns, and blood loss. More specifics can be gathered based on the nature of the sign in which the significant planets are placed. Thus Saturn in watery signs would produce drowning;

in Taurus, strangling or decapitation, etc. Similarly, Uranus in Gemini would produce accidents on short trips, railway, bicycle, or motor accidents, and similar occurrences.

Once you understand the simple nature of the planets, signs, and Houses, you will be able to easily determine their combinations. If I say that a certain fluid is H_2SO_4, anyone with an understanding of elementary chemistry will know that it is sulphuric acid, and similarly, if I say that a certain horoscope contains Saturn in Cancer in the Third House, which is astrologically expressed ♄ ♋ 3, anyone who has read the first pages of this book will be able to say: The subject should be cautious of short trips by water! It's all chemistry of a kind.

When the Fourth House contains benefic planets, or planets that throw good aspects to the luminaries, there will be peace and comfort in old age, or in the end of life. Neptune in the Fourth House shows withdrawal and separation, and when afflicting the luminaries or in evil aspect, it suggests death in a hospital, nursing home, or other place of isolation. Uranus in the Fourth, in similar conditions, denotes a sudden and unexpected death. Saturn similarly placed and aspected shows death in exile, deprivation, or great trouble. Mars in the Fourth House afflicting the luminaries or itself afflicted by other adverse planets denotes a violent death in the middle of conflict or death at war.

But a note of caution! It is wise to be careful in interpreting a subject's chart considering their death. In many instances it is better to leave them to find their own way.

THE STARS IN THEIR COURSES

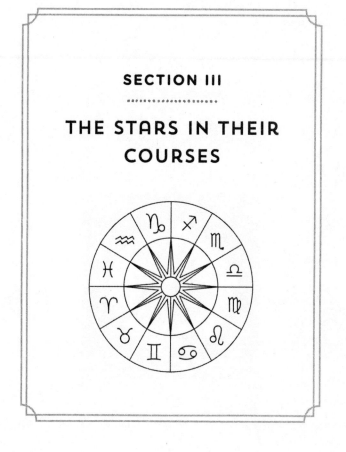

HOW TO SUMMARIZE A
HOROSCOPE

Before this book is concluded, it might be helpful for the reader if I outline a method for reading a complete horoscope. A horoscope should be read in the same order as the chapters of this book are laid out.

First, secure the chart of the subject based on their year, time, and location of birth.

The first step in reading the horoscope is to create a description of the primary personal traits of the subject, along with an evaluation of their constitution, physical health, disposition, and mental traits, considering these last two in relation to their state of health.

Next consider the conditions of their life: the

financial situation and outlook, position in life, occupation, relationships and love, and children. Then evaluate the role of travel in their life, and finally finish by considering the friends and enemies they will encounter. If the subject requests it, then you may also proceed to share insight into the nature of their death.

Be careful to fairly and impartially consider the evidence set before you in the natal chart. Planets that are at angles or are in elevation should be given special consideration because the nearer a planet is to the Midheaven, the greater its influence—for good or evil—will be on the life of the subject.

Read what you see, not what you imagine the subject's destiny should be. The less you know about the subject, the better. Though you will initially make some errors in judgment, if you carefully follow the rules in this book, these mistakes will become few and far between as you become familiar with the work. In the end the language of the horoscope will be so intelligible and clear it will interpret itself. You will be able to read the potential of a person's life as easily as you can read her face.

Once you're proficient at reading a birth chart,

you can proceed on to a more in-depth study of the mathematics of astrology, so that you can refine your general prognostics and make predictions that are clear, sharp, and to the point.

There is undoubtedly an element of intuitive perception involved in the reading of any horoscope, which will allow you to notice the small details and nuances of the chart. This is the difference between the rule of thumb worker and the inspirational reasoning of the intuitive worker. The first exhausts the books and the second embellishes them. This is true of every science in any arena. Books will take you up to a certain point of proficiency, and strictly following the principles of astrology will keep you within the bounds of safety. But if you are ever going to make a discovery or become a leading thinker in a field of science, you have to be gifted with what is called the "scientific imagination," which is simply another name for intuition. The same is true of astrology. Intuition is a powerful aspect of interpretation. But at no point does true intuition part company with exact reasoning. There is no separation between them; the one is an extension of the other. A higher form of reason argues from the known to the unknown. In this respect, a good astrologer is like the poet, "born, not made."

You will see that the more comfortable and familiar you are with the "book-learning" and technique of astrology, the more your intuition will be free to act. When a child is struggling with his multiplication tables, his appreciation of the binomial theorem or differential calculus is bound to be lacking. And, in the same way, a person who is still stuffing down the Alphabet of Astrology cannot be expected to intuit the potential of the Sun's direction to the quadrature of Saturn.

HOW TO BECOME A
SUCCESSFUL ASTROLOGER

I assume that nobody these days can afford to fritter away time on the study of useless subjects. In the unlikely case that one of my readers is interested in impractical knowledge, I'm afraid they will never be successful astrologers, because the first word of practical astrology is Utility. If the science didn't have a practical application for the affairs of everyday life, if, in short, it did not lead to the betterment of human life and thought, it would never have attracted the attention of Aristotle, Cicero, Galen, Claudius Ptolemy, Thales, and others of the old world, in addition to such people as Bacon, Cardan, Archbishop Usher, Naibod, Mercator, Ashmole, Kenelm Digby, Sir Christopher Heydon, Dryden, Dr. John Butler, Sir George Wharton,

Vincent Wing, George Witchel, Tycho Brahe, Kepler, and Flamstead of more recent biography. Regardless of what time period or country we consider, we can find a host of intelligent and even illustrious advocates in every area of life and learning. Suffice to say that the modern student of this ancient science is in very good company.

But what does astrology offer to the patient worker, the person who wishes to become a successful astrologer?

First and foremost, it will allow him to gain an insight into individual motive and character that no other science can possibly afford. It will enable him to know himself, his own strength and weakness, and prepare him to live harmoniously and justly with others. It will enhance his opportunities in life by revealing the benefic influences that are operating around him. It will serve as a warning when he approaches the quicksand and pitfalls in life. The able astrologer can discern her particular physical weaknesses, and be better equipped to avoid sickness. She will know whom to befriend and whom to avoid, and in selecting a partner in business or falling in love, she will be guided by a knowledge of the evil to avoid and the good things to pursue. She will choose her path in life with the confidence that her career is something she is well suited to and will succeed at. The astrologer will not be obsessed by ambitions that are beyond his power to achieve. He will learn to adapt to his environment, and will do his work in the world with the least possible friction and waste of energy. He will know when to guard against sickness and injury. The astrologer, guided by celestial knowledge, will not invest capital where there is nothing to be gained. She will see the end from the beginning. It may not make her a brilliant success in the world, but it will certainly save her from failure. She will understand the causes of inexplicable things, and know that some of the problems and struggles of life are not of her own making or require solutions. She will be content knowing that she is pursing the greatest potential of her horoscope. And finally, when her time comes to "shuffle off this mortal coil," she will be prepared, and will know that this death has been written in the stars since the moment of her birth. Astrology inevitably improves the lives of those who study it, helping them be of greater service to others and to the world at large.

To become a successful astrologer you must study patiently for several years, learning how the principles and ideas in this book and others work in reality. Once you are satisfied in your own mind that astrology is a dependable science and that you have a solid mastery of it, you must be generous in sharing it. You will run into those who believe, firmly, that the stars do not influence human affairs. Don't waste your time arguing about the logic behind astrology, but instead convince them by your predictions and interpretations.

A HELPFUL ILLUSTRATION

To demonstrate how to read a real horoscope, I will borrow the chart of a Mr. Joseph Chamberlain[2], who was born on the eighth of July, 1836, at Highbury, at 2:30 in the morning. Calculations have since enabled us to fix the exact time of birth as at 2 h. 36 m. a.m. His chart is on the following page.

The Constitution

In considering the constitution of Mr. Chamberlain, we must first consider the location of the Sun in his

---

2 Joseph Chamberlain was a leading political figure in England at the end of the nineteenth century. He started out a radical Liberal and ended up an imperialist, upsetting just about everyone in Parliament along the way.

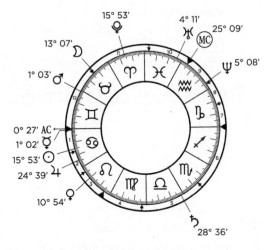

SUN IN CANCER, SECOND HOUSE
Sextile the Moon • Semisquare Mars • Conjunction Jupiter

MERCURY IN CANCER, FIRST HOUSE
Trine Uranus • Trine Saturn • Trine Midheaven

MARS IN GEMINI, SEVENTH HOUSE
Square Uranus • Semisquare Sun • Trine Neptune • Square Midheaven • Conjunction Saturn and Moon

MOON IN TAURUS, SEVENTH HOUSE
Square Venus • Sextile Sun • Square Neptune

URANUS IN PISCES, TENTH HOUSE
Trine Mercury • Square Mars • Trine Saturn • Conjunction Midheaven

MIDHEAVEN, AQUARIUS

NEPTUNE IN AQUARIUS, NINTH HOUSE
Opposite Venus • Trine Mars • Square Saturn • Square Moon

SATURN IN LIBRA, FIFTH HOUSE
Trine Mercury • Trine Midheaven • Square Jupiter • Trine Uranus •
Square Neptune

VENUS IN LEO, THIRD HOUSE
Square Moon • Opposite Neptune

JUPITER IN CANCER, SECOND HOUSE
Square Saturn

chart. In this case, with Gemini as his rising sign, and the Sun in near conjunction with Jupiter and in close sextile to the Moon, there is little doubt that the late Colonial Secretary was gifted with an excellent constitution. The sextile of the luminaries is a powerful element, and whenever sickness does appear there will be a speedy recovery. The semisquare aspect of Mars suggests problems with the hands and feet and predisposes him to accidents and wounds to the right shoulder or clavicle. But it will also give him a strong vital energy and a good resistance to disease.

The rising sign, Gemini, gives nervous energy and an enormous capacity for work, which is due to nervous tension supported by a sound vitality. The only potential hereditary issues suggested in this chart are indicated by Mars, which predisposes one to fevers, and to issues due to acidity.

The Health

The Moon is the deciding factor in questions of health and sickness. In this chart, the Moon is strong in the sign Taurus, but not particularly well placed in the Twelfth House. More importantly, it is in negative aspect (square) with both Neptune and Venus, which are located in fixed signs (Aquarius and Leo, respectively). These point to functional disorders of the heart, throat, and excretory system (see page 45). On the other hand, the Moon is in the good aspects to the Sun, Jupiter, and Uranus to counteract these potential health issues. The good aspect between the Moon and Sun, in particular, indicates that he will enjoy speedy recovery from illnesses, and we can predict that he will enjoy considerable immunity from serious sicknesses.

Character and Disposition

In considering Mr. Chamberlain's overall disposition (pages 52–53), we can first notice that the majority of the planets are in cardinal signs, with three planets (including the Moon) in fixed signs. This indicates a character that is energetic, ambitious, active, sharp, ingenious, lively, and persevering; capable of forging a path for himself in life and making headway against obstacles; disposed to ride roughshod over anyone who opposes him; gifted with a pioneering spirit and incisive manner and disposed at times to do what he wants regardless of the feelings and opinions of others. At the same time there is sufficient patience, method, caution, and watchfulness to make this extreme sense of purpose very effective. Hard working, firm (at times stubborn), systematic, and self-reliant, he is capable of waiting for opportunities. He is a force to be reckoned with.

However, he lacks adaptability, charm, and the ability to empathize with the feelings of others. He is too ambitious to be self-centered, but also too focused to be sympathetic.

In this chart, we find Mercury in trine aspect to both Saturn and Uranus (page 53). This gives considerable mental capacity, a thorough grasp of the facts, and a businesslike mind; some originality, creativity, patience, caution, and secrecy. Though there is some imagination due to the influence of Uranus, it does not define his character and his sympathies are not wide. His methods and actions are governed by literal fact and mathematical certainty. He devours what is accessible. He takes the small fish by the handful and makes a meal of them; but he leaves the ponderous whales for those of greater imagination and more leisurely inclination.

Finally, we consider the planets located in the Third and Ninth Houses. And here we see that inspiration is by no means absent. The presence of Neptune in the Ninth House in trine to the rising Mercury is a mark of inventive genius, acute mental perception, and a keen eye for making sense of the future. Venus in the Third House indicates some artistic taste, and a considerable appreciation of art and culture. But the two angular influences of Uranus and Mercury are the most dominant aspects, giving him a mathematical mind and creating a precise, businesslike, energetic, and magnetic personality.

Finance

The position of the Sun in conjunction with Jupiter in the Second House and sextile to the Moon is a strong sign of good fortune and prosperity. In regard to Mr. Chamberlain's horoscope, we can notice that Jupiter, which is so powerful financially when located in the Second House as we see here, is also the ruler of the Seventh. This suggests that partnerships, whether commercial or social, that he engages in will be profitable from a monetary point of view. This is underscored by the fact that the Moon is positively affected by the good aspect of the Sun in the Second House.

Position

To consider the subject's status and position in the world, we begin by considering the overall locations of the planets (page 63). All the planets except Neptune and Saturn are rising, and this clearly indicates a man who desires honor and independence and will achieve those things.

Uranus in the Midheaven and close to the meridian indicates the association with civic and governmental bodies (page 34) that has defined Mr. Chamberlain's work. Whereas the trine aspect of Mercury in the Ascendant to Uranus in the Midheaven and the sextile of the Moon to Uranus are sure indications of popularity, the square aspect of

Mars to Uranus from the Twelfth House indicates strong enemies and rivals.

Marriage

Mr. Chamberlain has been married three times. In considering his chart, you will notice that not only is there a double-bodied sign on the cusp of the Seventh House (in this case Sagittarius), but the Moon also applies to both the Sun and Jupiter in the sign Cancer. Since the aspect of the Moon is benefic to both the Sun and Jupiter, the marriages should be harmonious and fortunate. It is well known that Mr. Chamberlain has, from a worldly point of view, married advantageously. Perhaps, as they say, everything is clearer in hindsight, but I would mention that this particular confluence of planets occurred long before I started reading it and the rules I am using to untangle it were written by Ptolemy in the second century. So perhaps this observation isn't so late after all. Saturn's negative aspect to Jupiter, the ruler of the Seventh House, combined with the Moon in negative aspect with Venus (page 73) give us hints as to the successive losses that have troubled his romantic life.

Children

The position of Saturn, a malefic, in the Fifth House, and Venus in negative aspect with both Neptune and the Moon, all suggest a small family.

In this chart, Venus is the ruler, jointly with Mercury, of the Fifth House (since the Fifth House is positioned in both Libra and Virgo which are ruled by Venus and Mercury), while Saturn is in the Fifth and ruler of the Eighth House. These positions and aspects threaten a negative influence on the children.

The position of Mercury, joint ruler of the Fifth, in the sign Cancer, and just about to rise in the horoscope, promises honors and distinction to the first-born.

Traveling

The Moon and Mars are cadent in the horoscope, and Mercury, the "winged messenger" (symbol of the trading ship), is rising. These are indications of many journeys and changes and constant unrest. But the fact that the fixed signs are located on the cusps of the Third and Ninth Houses, with the Moon also in a fixed sign, indicates that Mr. Chamberlain is not a long-distance traveler.

Friends and Enemies

It was the boast of Bismarck that he was the "best-hated man in Europe," and it would be strange if Mr. Chamberlain did not have his own fair share of enemies. Nevertheless, there are only two aspects in this horoscope that seem to point to trouble in that area. In this case, that is Neptune, which afflicts both the Moon and Venus, and Mars, which afflicts Uranus in the Midheaven and the Sun in the Second House (see page 88).

By referring these two points to the Ecliptic we find they correspond to the Sun's position on or about the twenty-fourth of May, and the twenty-sixth of January, and I shall leave you to consider whose birthdays might correspond with those dates.

Mr. Chamberlain will not find himself lacking in friends. With the Moon in sextile to the Sun and Jupiter, the ruler of the Eleventh House, in a benefic relationship with the Moon, he would always be able to count on a friendly face. The only negative indication is that Mars, part ruler of the Eleventh House (since the Eleventh House resides in Aries which is ruled by Mars), is located in the Twelfth House and is in square aspect to Uranus in the Midheaven. This can be interpreted to mean that some of his friends will likely become his enemies and will work ineffectually against him. Why ineffectually? Because Mercury, the ruler of the Ascendant and prime significator of Mr. Chamberlain, is angular and well aspected, while Mars is weak and afflicted by Uranus which is in elevation above it.

Conclusion

The fame and position Mr. Chamberlain has attained in the political world is not solely due to the benefic position of the principal planets in his horoscope. Opportunity is not everything. The ability and will to use it is equally important.

QUICK REFERENCE GUIDE

I n this newly updated edition of the book, we've taken the liberty of adding a brief reference guide to Sepharial's original work. Here you'll find some of the most important facts and points from the book all gathered together for easy reference as you begin to interpret horoscopes on your own. Consider it your cheat sheet to the secrets of the stars.

The Luminaries and Planets

The Sun ☉
Moon ☽
Neptune ♆

Uranus ♅
Saturn ♄
Jupiter ♃
Mars ♂
Venus ♀
Mercury ☿

The Natures of the Planets

Neptune: chaos, confusion, deception

Uranus: eccentricity, originality, estrangement

Saturn: lack, obstacles, denial

Jupiter: affluence, fruitfulness, increase

Sun: recognition, honor

Mars: excess, impulse, quarreling

Venus: peace, happiness, agreement

Mercury: commerce, versatility, adaptability

Moon: changes, attention

Neptune acts upon the mind of man to create a highly strung nervous temperament that can result in great genius or in instability. It creates complications in business and other involved or complicated matters. It influences one towards fraud, double-dealing, and irresponsible actions. In the body it produces a gaunt frame and weak lungs.

Uranus gives an eccentric mind, waywardness, originality, inventiveness. In business, it produces sudden and unexpected developments, irregularities, instability, and unexpected turns of good and bad fortune. In the body, it's related to the nervous system, and its diseases are paralysis, lesions or ulcers, and nerve issues.

Saturn produces a thoughtful, sober, dignified mind; steadfastness, patience, and endurance; along with a disposition to routine and habit. In financial affairs it gives steady results that are equivalent to the effort exerted, success that is slow but sure, but also hardship, lack, and difficulty. In the body it is related to the bones, and its effects are brought about by blockages, chills, and inhibition of function.

Jupiter gives joviality, optimism, bountifulness, generosity, a rich and fruitful mind. It renders the subject fortunate in his affairs, giving success and often wealth. When this planet is a strong presence in the horoscope a person is never washed out. In the body it is related to the arteries and blood flow, and its diseases are those that are a result of excess, over-indulgence, and congestion.

Mars confers a sense of freedom, much ambition and executive ability, frankness, truthfulness, and a disregard for consequences. It renders the mind force-ful and militant, inclined to pursue new projects and ideas. In the body it is related to the muscular system. Its diseases are those associated with inflammation.

Venus confers poetry, good taste, refinement, artistic sense, gentleness, docility, and a love of pleasure. It renders the business both pleasant and prosperous, creating profit from both artistic and practical pursuits. Next to Jupiter it has the most positive effects. In the body it has relation to the venous system, and its dis-eases are blood-related ones that arise from impuri-ties of the blood: eczema, smallpox, measles, etc.

Mercury renders its subjects active, versatile, capa-ble and businesslike, disposed to commerce, whether of the mind or the market, eager in the pursuit of knowledge, alert, and well-informed. Its influence on daily life is variable, because it always translates the nature of that planet that it is most near. In the body it is related to the senses and to the reflexes.

The Moon gives charisma and gracefulness, an

adaptable nature, variableness, love of change, romance, and adventure; a love for exploration and travel. In the body it corresponds to the glandular system, and its diseases are related to the lymphatic glands and vascular tissue.

The Sun makes its subjects magnanimous, noble, proud, honest and disdainful of immoral actions, loyal, truthful, and fearless. It produces honor and success for officials, and makes the subject fortunate in their affairs. In the body it controls the life force.

The Signs

1. Aries, the Ram ♈
2. Taurus, the Bull ♉
3. Gemini, the Twins ♊
4. Cancer, the Crab ♋
5. Leo, the Lion ♌
6. Virgo, the Virgin ♍
7. Libra, the Balance ♎
8. Scorpio, the Scorpion ♏
9. Sagittarius, the Hunter ♐
10. Capricorn, the Goat ♑

11. Aquarius, the Waterman ♒
12. Pisces, the Fishes ♓

Fire—Aries, Leo, Sagittarius
Earth—Taurus, Virgo, Capricorn
Air—Gemini, Libra, Aquarius
Water—Cancer, Scorpio, Pisces

Modality

Cardinal—Aries, Cancer, Libra, Capricorn
Fixed—Taurus, Leo, Scorpio, Aquarius
Mutable—Gemini, Virgo, Sagittarius, Pisces

Double-Bodied Signs

Gemini, Sagittarius, and Pisces

Rulers

Saturn governs Aquarius and Capricorn
Jupiter governs Pisces and Sagittarius
Mars governs Aries and Scorpio

Venus governs Taurus and Libra

Mercury governs Gemini and Virgo

The Moon governs Cancer

The Sun governs Leo

The Houses

The First House governs personal appearance, but specifically the face and head.

The Second House rules over finance, material possessions, commerce, and work. In the body it governs the neck and throat.

The Third House governs short journeys, communication, family, and neighbors. In the body it governs the arms and lungs.

The Fourth House governs real estate, the home, plants, mothers and motherhood, and the end of life. In the body, the breasts and thorax.

The Fifth House rules over children, sex, romantic relationships, and social pleasures. In the body, the back and heart.

The Sixth House governs health, personal comforts, clothes, food, and other necessities, sanitation, and hygiene. In the body it rules over the abdomen and lower organs.

The Seventh House has dominion over marriage, contracts, agreements, partners, and business relationships. In the body it is related to the reproductive organs and kidneys.

The Eighth House rules death, loss, inheritances, and matters relating to the deceased. In the body it is related to the excretory system.

The Ninth House is said to govern long journeys, writing and books, religious beliefs, foreign lands, and legal affairs. In the body it rules the thighs.

The Tenth House rules over position and reputation, honor and fame, the father, and authority figures. In the body it rules over the knees.

The Eleventh House governs friends, social groups, and clubs or companies the subject is associated with. In the body it is related to the legs from calf to ankle.

The Twelfth House rules ambushes, restraints, difficulties, imprisonment, confinement, and all limitations of personal freedom. In the body it rules the ankles and feet.

Angular or Cardinal Houses

The First, Fourth, Seventh, and Tenth

Aspects

Semisquare	45 degrees	Evil/Negative
Sextile	60 degrees	Good/Positive
Square	90 degrees	Evil/Negative
Trine	120 degrees	Good/Positive
Sesquiquadrate	135 degrees	Evil/Negative
Opposition	180 degrees	Evil/Negative

Benefic Planets: Jupiter, Venus, Sun, Moon, and Mercury (when well aspected or in a friendly sign)

Malefic Planets: Neptune, Uranus, Saturn, and Mars, Mercury (when poorly aspected or in an unfriendly sign)

Significators

Moon: the mother, female relationships, personal health and fortune

Sun: the father, male relationships, the vital principle, and status

Mercury: the mind and intellect, and the senses in general

Venus: love affairs, domestic relations, pleasure, and young female relationships, sisters, etc.

Mars: enterprises, conflict, and young male relations

Jupiter: wealth and profit

Saturn: inheritances and elderly people

Uranus: civic and governmental bodies

Neptune: journeys and psychic experiences

RESOURCES

https://cafeastrology.com/glossaryofastrology.html
Glossary of astrological terms

https://www.astrotheme.com
Provides an extensive selection of horoscopes for
    various celebrities, including the illustrious Mr.
    Chamberlain profiled in this book.

There are countless places online to easily download
    your own chart, or that of a friend. Some of
    them include:
https://justastrologythings.com/pages/chart
https://astro.cafeastrology.com/natal.php
https://www.costarastrology.com/natal-chart

ABOUT THE AUTHOR

Sepharial was a pen name for Walter Gornold, an influential astrologer in the nineteenth century. Born in 1864 in England, Gornold was the editor of *Old Moore's Almanac* and was one of the founding members of the Theosophical movement in England.

ABOUT THE FOREWORD AUTHOR

June Rifkin is the coauthor of several books, including *The Complete Book of Astrology*, *The One World Tarot*, and *Signature for Success: How Handwriting Can Influence Your Career, Your Relationships, and Your Life*. Her published play, *Separation Anxiety*, is featured in *One on One: The Best Women's Monologues of the 21st Century*. June also serves as a freelance editor and literary consultant working closely with many notables in astrology, tarot, Wicca, and psychic mediumship.